HAIRS AND GRACES

One-Woman Drama

For Stage

By

Cazz Anders

Published by Cazz Anders

STAMFORD

UK

Cover illustrations by Jojo

Printed by Kindle Direct Publishing

United Kingdom

ACT ONE

Interior of a traditional hairdressing salon – 2 basins, 3 chairs with old-fashioned canopy dryers. There's a reception desk to one side, with a dog in a basket on the floor. In one corner, by the windows, there's a small Christmas tree with coloured lights. The desk and all available surfaces are covered with used glasses, plates, cups and saucers.

Scene One

As the curtain rises we see **JOSIE** *a 62-year-old divorcee who is a hairdresser in a small market town. Her bleached-blonde hair is piled high and she wears bright leggings and a blouse with prints of dogs.*

Josie shuts the shop door and turns the sign to 'closed'. She starts to tidy up, collecting sherry glasses, and cups and saucers.

JOSIE. Well, I didn't think we'd see the back of Mrs Mason, did you? If I never have to hear about her daughter's operation again, it'll be too soon. And Miss Ward! She can't half knock it back. I was only saying to Mavis in the post office the other day – that'll be how she's got to 91. Pickled. Still, she needs something to live for, I suppose.

Josie sees several glasses still half full of sherry.

Oh my, what a waste – do they think I'm made of money? Decent bit of stuff too – none of your supermarket rubbish. All my ladies are grateful for a bit of festive cheer when they're under the dryers – all except Mrs Harris, of course.

(mimics faux-posh voice) 'Oh no, Josie. Wouldn't dream of *English* – not the same when you've been used to 'the real thing'.'

Cheeky cow. Just 'cos her Stanley's spending his inheritance on a villa in Spain. Old Man Harris'll be spinning in his grave. Not even cold before they'd sold the shop.

They *said* that there's no call for a hardware shop any more. Anything broken and it's on the tip. Well, they can blame IKEA all they like, but I remember that Stanley Harris at school. Stuck up, he was. All airs and graces because his dad owned the shop. And *her* – she just loves being the centre of attention – all that cloak and dagger stuff about who's bought it.
She was only doing it so I'd ask.
Well, wasn't giving her the satisfaction.

Josie looks at the glasses lined up on the desk.

Hmm, shame to waste it.
She tips the left-over sherry into one glass and takes a sip.

Now, give me five minutes and we'll go walkies. And din-dins. What do you fancy for your din-dins? I think we might have a bit of your special steak left. C'mon then, let's get cracking.

Josie picks up dog lead.

Blackout.

Scene Two

Five weeks later - interior of the salon. Rain outside windows.

The Christmas tree has gone and there's a large vase of lilies on the desk. Dog is still in the basket.

JOSIE. Always a bit quiet in January.
(pause)

Still, as I was saying to Mavis, we had some excitement last week. Lovely young man came in. I reckon he was from The Mercury. You know what these undercover reporters are like; he'll be sussing out the local businesses for the Awards. I wonder who nominated me. Could be anyone really.
Well, anyway. *Said* he wanted to pick my brains about being a hairdresser. *Said* he was thinking about it as a career, but he didn't pull the wool over *my* eyes. The pad and pen gave him away – taking all those notes.

I think he was grateful for the welcome, really. Must be awful trying to interview people without them guessing what you're up to.
Hmm, wonder if I should get a new frock for the ceremony.

He was here ages – and he wolfed down my Victoria sandwich even if he did complain there was no cream. Ethan, I said, I've made more WI cakes than you've had hot dinners and it comes with raspberry jam. No strawberries, no butter filling and certainly no cream. I know a jam sponge nearly as well as I know my Ladies. I know what works and I stick to it.

Soon as I mentioned them, he was very interested to hear all about my Ladies. He wasn't giving any hints about who's voted for me, just seemed keen to know who likes what, who the nice ones are, who's a moaner. I told him, when you've been doing hair as long as I have, you get to know all their little foibles. And none of my *clientele* "moan". *(Josie makes speech marks with her fingers)* They're all as happy as Larry. Been with me for years.

Josie gets up and goes to the window.

Looks like the rain's easing up a bit – let's go and have a nose at Harris's. See if we can work out who's bought it. Hope it's a green-grocers, we could do with a bit of fresh fruit and veg around here. Or how about a Pet Shop? Something to tempt you while you're off your food?

Josie bends to pat the dog.

Blackout.

Scene Three

Six weeks later – interior of the salon. Bright sunshine outside.

There's a vase of tulips on the desk.

Josie leafs through the local paper.

JOSIE. Still no sign of the Awards. As I said to Mavis when I saw her in the newsagents, I did think that young man would at least have kept me up to date.

Ooh, look! 'Grand Opening' 17 Market Square – that's Harris's. They've done very well to keep it under wraps – no hint of what's coming. Mrs Mason reckons it's going to be one of those Adult Shops. Don't be ridiculous, I said to her – there's no call for ***that*** round here, but she says she's seen a man coming and going. That doesn't mean anything, I told her, but she's convinced that wearing black leather trousers means he's into a bit of hanky-panky. Stupid woman. I bet it'll be a trendy clothes shop – you know the sort, music so loud you can't hear yourself think and so dark inside, you think there's been a power cut. Not my cup of tea, but they seem to be all the rage with the kids today.

Right, my darling, we've got a bit of time before Miss Ward rolls in, fancy a potter round the park?

Oh, come on, you lazy thing – you can't stay in bed all day.

Blackout.

Curtain.

ACT TWO

Interior of the salon. There's a tall vase of delphiniums and gladioli on the desk. The salon is deserted and very tidy.

Scene One

The curtain rises and we see **JOSIE** *standing at the desk, telephone receiver in one hand.*

JOSIE. Well, we *are* rather busy, but I can squeeze you in just after lunch… Yes, of course. What's the name again? Oh… No, we don't have a male stylist, I'm afraid. I'm the Proprietor and I'll be taking care of you personally…

No, as I said, we don't have a man here. What was your name? Hello? Hello?

Got cut off. Honestly, I'll be giving BT what for. Having nothing but trouble with the line. Must be something wrong with the exchange – Mrs Mason hasn't called to cancel, and she'd never not turn up. I'm the only one who knows how she likes her perm. 'You're a marvel with those rollers, Josie,' she always says to me. Can't think where she's got to. I was looking forward to a chat.

Haven't had chance to talk to Mavis much. She always seems to be in a rush these days. I wanted to fill her in about The Man. The one who took over at Harris's. *(pause)* Only it's not a green-grocers, or a pet shop. It's 'Ethan's Emporium' now. Calls himself a *stylist.* He's giving them Indian Head Massages and deep-heat conditioner, and Miss Ward says he told her he's got massage chairs at the basins. Massage chairs! I ask you – maybe Mrs Mason wasn't that far off the mark!

And the rep from Elliott's says he's not using her at all. Into all these highfalutin brands. I said to her, none of my Ladies will be prepared to pay for Kerastase. We've got on perfectly well for years with good old Salon Selectives and there's no reason for them to change now. He'll be out of business before he knows it. Got off on the wrong foot with me, too. Pretending to be a journalist! I'll be giving him a piece of my mind when I see him.

Anyway, I'm sure we'll have a proper catch-up when Mavis is back from her hols. She must be off soon – surprised she hasn't been in.

Josie looks out of the window.

Is that her coming out of the butchers?

Josie knocks on the glass.

Mavis! Mavis!

No, she can't hear me. Don't think it could have been her anyway, we haven't done her colour for ages.

Blackout.

Scene Two

Interior of the salon. Rain.

There's a vase of chrysanthemums and ox-eye daisies on the desk.

Josie sits at the desk.

JOSIE. Well, that's a turn up for the books. Apparently, The Man's spitting tacks because his order hasn't turned up for the third month in a row. He's had to put Mavis off so he can go down to the Wholesalers. He had to cancel everyone last week too when they thought that gas pipe had burst.

I'm surprised Mavis had the nerve to come and ask me to do her but I must say, her roots are really starting to show. Pity I couldn't get her in before her birthday party. She thinks I don't know about the party, but I overheard Mrs Mason saying her Sharon was going to have to take her own food, on account of her operation. It's a Curry Night so I wouldn't have wanted to go anyway.

We'll have a cosy night in. Just you, me and Strictly, and we'll see if you can manage a bit of chicken.

Blackout.

Scene Three

Interior of the salon – it's dark outside.

The dog basket has gone and there's an Urn on the counter. It's in the shape of a dog with a bone on top. There are no flowers. **JOSIE** *is wearing a shapeless navy jumper and her hair is lank on her shoulders.*

JOSIE. Nothing's gone right since *he* came.

She holds the urn to her chest.

Oh, my darling, what am I going to do? If it gets into papers, even Miss Ward will go to *him.*

Having a policeman through the door was horrible. Thought he was a customer to start with. (*She sighs.*) Should've known better.

Don't know what they're doing - allowing kids on the force anyway. He looked about 12, bet he hasn't even started shaving.

(mimics pompous, deep voice) 'Madam, we have reason to believe that you've been interfering with a business on The Square.' Well, I told him straight out – if you've got any evidence, then arrest me. I'm an upstanding member of this Community – all my Ladies'll tell you that. He said he'd already spoken to them –and they're *The Man's* Ladies now, which

is why the finger of suspicion has been pointed at me. 'Do your worst' I told him and held out my wrists to be handcuffed. Impudent upstart told me not to be so melodramatic and that he was only making enquiries. I gave him pretty short shrift at that – he'd just accused me right out! He back-tracked smartish and mumbled something about being on Probation and needing to impress the bigwigs. You won't get far, persecuting innocent old ladies, I told him. He got all tongue-tied after that, poor boy, so I sent him on his way with a piece of cake.

(pause)

But there's no way they could know I had anything to do with cancelling his Redken orders, and I swear I *could* smell gas outside his salon. Not my fault the gas board had to dig up the pavement outside to see if they could find anything. And any of those lads who hang around at night could have switched off his water – those mains covers are very flimsy. They could have done it for a laugh.

Josie puts the urn back on the desk.

Oh, don't look at me like that. I'll stop, I promise.

No point anymore anyway. Might as well shut up shop for good – it's just not the same without you.

Blackout.

Curtain.

ACT THREE

Exterior – front of the salon. The windows are whited out and all the signage has gone. A large camper van is parked outside, covered in a white silk sheet.

Scene One

As the curtain rises we see **JOSIE** *in Dalmatian-print leggings and a frilly blouse. Her hair is even blonder and more buoyant than before.*

JOSIE. They've taken me off the tablets. I was worried at first that I wouldn't be able to manage without them, but doctor said I'd be fine, and she was right. She was right about the counselling too. Talking things through really helps. A problem shared is a problem halved, they say. And it's true.

I've made up with Mavis as well – she was ever so sorry. 'A friend in need is a friend indeed,' she said, 'and I wasn't a very good friend, Josie.' I told her not to worry, because in my experience, a friend in need is a bloody nuisance. Oh, how we laughed. I'd forgotten how much we used to laugh….

(pause)

Anyway! I've sorted things out with Ethan too. He's not bad when you get to know him – bit flamboyant for my taste and those leather trousers leave nothing to the imagination. I can see why Mrs Mason got ideas…

He's bought the shop. Going to turn it into a Beauty Salon and Day Spa, whatever that is when it's at home. Gave me the asking price for it, no argument. Makes me wonder if I should have asked more… But that doesn't matter because it's more than paid for this.

Josie gestures to the white sheet.

Big unveiling at 3 o'clock, but you can have a sneak preview if you like. I thought about a cake shop to start with, but I knew in my heart-of-hearts. There's only one thing I've ever *really* wanted to do.

She pulls aside the sheet with a flourish, to reveal a white campervan, with large black paw-prints all over it.

Ta-dah! Welcome to Posh Paws Poochie Parlour! From Pampered Pugs to Dirty Dalmatians, if you have a canine companion in need of cossetting, you know where to come. Yeah, I know…bit of a mouthful – but it looks fantastic on the leaflets.

Josie climbs into the driver's seat and pushes a button. A loud barking comes over the tannoy on the roof – rather like an old-fashioned ice-cream van.

Mavis is going to be my assistant. We've already had enquiries from all over the place and we've got some big ideas. Did you know, Redken have a line in Poochie Perms?

Nah – only joking.... but it's worth a thought!

THE END

Printed in Great Britain
by Amazon

78498566R00020